STEALTH TECHNOLOGY

BY ELIZABETH NOLL

BELLWETHER MEDIA • MINNEAPOLIS, MN

™

Torque brims with excitement
perfect for thrill-seekers of all kinds.
Discover daring survival skills, explore
uncharted worlds, and marvel at mighty
engines and extreme sports. In *Torque* books,
anything can happen. Are you ready?

Library of Congress Cataloging-in-Publication Data

LC record for Stealth Technology available at: https://lccn.loc.gov/2021051721

Editor: Betsy Rathburn   Designer: Jeffrey Kollock

Printed in the United States of America, North Mankato, MN.

TABLE OF CONTENTS

BIRD OR PLANE?

F-35 LIGHTNING II

A black plane zooms across the night sky.
It looks like a hawk ready to attack!
People on the ground see only flashing lights.

Enemy soldiers watch their **radar** screens.
But the screens show only a small dot.
The plane used stealth technology to hide!

RADAR SCREENS

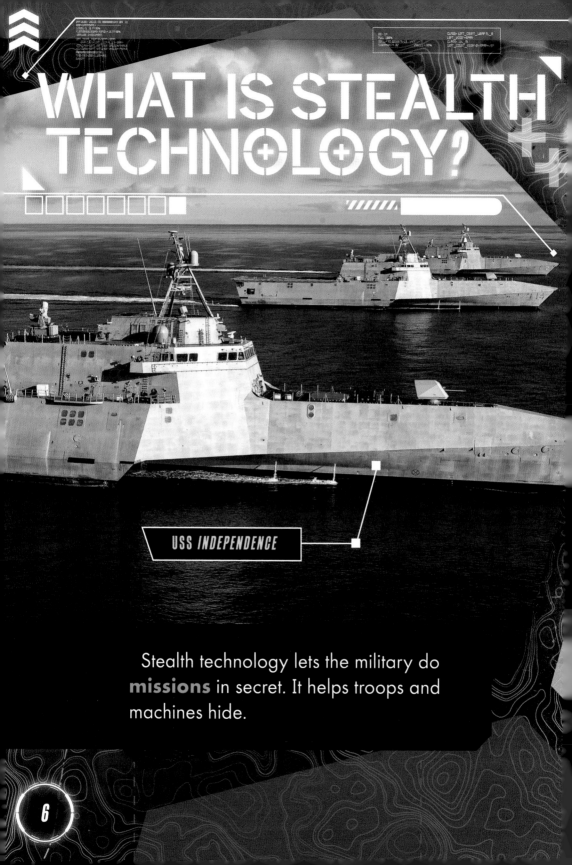

WHAT IS STEALTH TECHNOLOGY?

USS *INDEPENDENCE*

Stealth technology lets the military do **missions** in secret. It helps troops and machines hide.

Troops use it to sneak into enemy **territory**.
They also fly planes to spy on military bases.
Enemies cannot spot stealth weapons or vehicles!

MORE PLANES

The United States had 540 stealth planes in 2020. That is over 10 times more than any other country!

B-2 SPIRIT

Camouflage is one of the most common uses of stealth. It helps people and machines blend into surroundings. Soldiers may wear camouflage clothing. Vehicles may be painted in different colors and patterns.

Camouflage has also been used to trick enemies. Some ships were painted in bold patterns during World War I. Enemies did not know where to attack!

CAMOUFLAGE PATTERN

TIMELINE

1700s
FIRST KNOWN CAMOUFLAGE

1917
DAZZLE CAMOUFLAGE

EARLY 1980s
F-117 NIGHTHAWK

1998
CHALLENGER 2 TANK

2006
F-35 LIGHTNING II

2013
USS *ZUMWALT*

New technology can easily spot troops and machines. The military must find new ways to hide. Some vehicles have special shapes. They are hard for radar and **sonar** tools to spot.

F-22 RAPTOR

BOXER

STEALTH PROFILE

MARK 8 SEAL DELIVERY VEHICLE

DEVELOPED: 1970s

FEATURES: UNDERWATER VEHICLE MADE WITH SPECIAL COATINGS TO ESCAPE SONAR TOOLS

The military also uses special coatings on planes and ships. They help escape radar and sonar!

THE SCIENCE BEHIND STEALTH TECHNOLOGY

Radar easily spots vehicles with pointed parts. Stealth vehicles have special shapes to hide from radar. Some planes and ships have rounded curves. Others have flat **panels**.

HOW STEALTH PLANES WORK

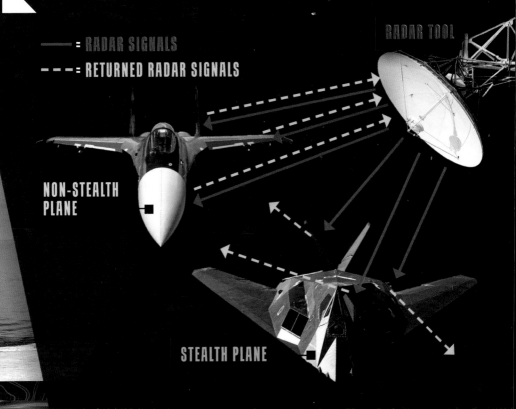

= RADAR SIGNALS

---= RETURNED RADAR SIGNALS

RADAR TOOL

NON-STEALTH PLANE

STEALTH PLANE

The shapes make radar **signals** bounce in different directions. They do not go back to enemies!

Special coatings also help vehicles hide from radar. Some vehicles are covered in **RAMs**.

USS *COLORADO*

5

RAMs soak up most radar signals.
Fewer signals bounce back to enemies.
The vehicle looks much smaller on radar screens.
Enemies might think big planes are small birds!

RAM

INFRARED VISION

INFRARED DEVICE

Military vehicles can also be spotted on **infrared devices**. These tools find things that are hotter than what is around them. They easily spot gas from engines.

Some stealth vehicles mix cool air with hot gas. Others spread heat over a large area. Infrared tools cannot spot these vehicles!

QUIET FLYING

Stealth aircraft cannot be too loud. Some have engines inside of the plane. This makes them quieter!

THE FUTURE OF STEALTH TECHNOLOGY

Future military vehicles may be even harder to spot. One company is working on vehicles that appear invisible!

TANK WITH ADAPTIV TILES

NEW BOMBER

The B-21 Raider is planned for release in the 2020s. This stealth plane is big enough to carry a powerful bomb!

FUTURE STEALTH PROFILE

TANK USING ADAPTIV CAMOUFLAGE

ADAPTIV CAMOUFLAGE

DEVELOPED: INTRODUCED IN 2011

FEATURES: HIDES VEHICLES FROM INFRARED DEVICES BY CHANGING TEMPERATURE

Special tiles will cover the vehicles. The tiles change the vehicles' temperatures to match their surroundings. This helps them escape being spotted. The tiles could also change colors or patterns to blend in.

Stealth planes may someday have **morphing wings**. These wings are made of many tiny parts. They have no joints or flaps. Radar cannot easily spot them. The wings change shape when the plane changes direction or speed.

NON-MILITARY USES

BUILDING

STEALTH MATERIALS

PUBLIC SAFETY

INFRARED DEVICES

HUNTING

CAMOUFLAGE

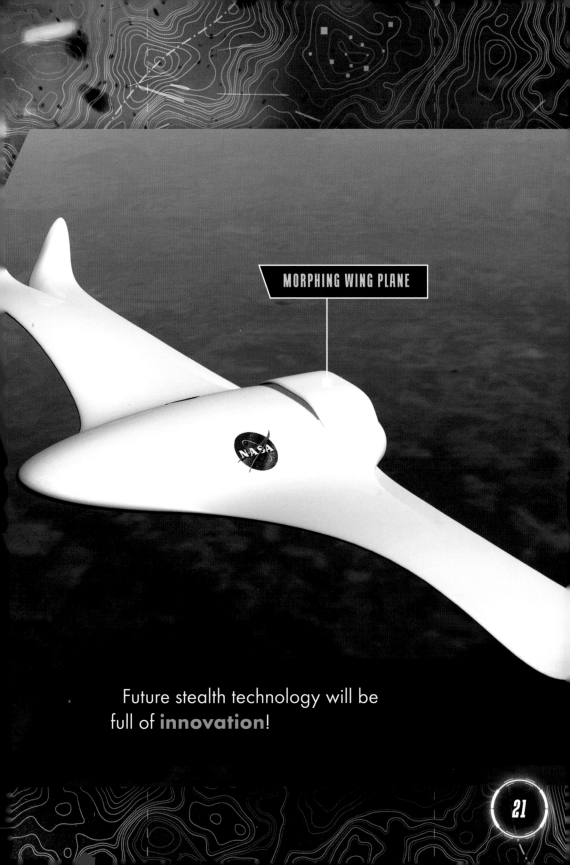

MORPHING WING PLANE

Future stealth technology will be full of **innovation**!

GLOSSARY

camouflage—the use of special patterns and colors to hide something by making it look like its surroundings

infrared devices—tools that can pick up on and show heat

innovation—the development of new ideas and methods

missions—jobs to complete a certain task

morphing wings—wings that change shape when an airplane changes speed or direction

panels—flat parts

radar—related to a tool that uses radio waves to spot tanks, planes, and other vehicles

RAMs—radar absorbent materials; RAMs are special coatings used to help vehicles avoid being spotted.

signals—information sent and received

sonar—related to a tool that uses sound waves to find things underwater

territory—an area controlled by a specific person or group

AT THE LIBRARY

Barton, Chris. *Dazzle Ships: World War I and the Art of Confusion.* Minneapolis, Minn.: Millbrook Press, 2017.

Hustad, Douglas. *U.S. Army Equipment and Vehicles.* Minneapolis, Minn.: Abdo Publishing, 2021.

Noll, Elizabeth. *Surveillance.* Minneapolis, Minn.: Bellwether Media, 2022.

ON THE WEB

FACTSURFER

Factsurfer.com gives you a safe, fun way to find more information.

1. Go to www.factsurfer.com

2. Enter "stealth technology" into the search box and click Q.

3. Select your book cover to see a list of related content.

INDEX